Having Once Paused

Having Once Paused

Poems of Zen Master Ikkyū (1394–1481)

Translated by Sarah Messer and Kidder Smith

UNIVERSITY OF MICHIGAN PRESS

Ann Arbor

Published in the United States of America by
the University of Michigan Press
Printed and bound by CPI Group (UK) Ltd, Croydon, CR0 4YY

2018   2017   2016   2015   4   3   2   1

A CIP catalog record for this book is available from the British Library.

ISBN 978-0-472-07256-9 (hardcover)
ISBN 978-0-472-05256-1 (paper)
ISBN 978-0-472-12095-6 (e-book)

for t.k. and s.t.

only because of,
impossible without

Contents

Translators' Introduction   1

A Note on the Word Fūryū,
Translation, and the Art of Magic,
by Traktung Yeshe Dorje   9

The poems:

     I. Lineage   11

     II. Fūryū   45

     III. Hunger   67

     IV. Mori   91

Notes and References   123

Further Reading   129

Authors   131

Translators' Introduction

Ikkyū is unique in Zen for letting his love of all appearance occupy him until it destroys any possibility for safety or seclusion. In his poetry, he turns the eye of enlightenment to all phenomena: politics, pine trees, hard meditation practice, sex, wine. The poems express the unborn bliss of his realization and equally his devastation at the horrors of this world. From this union of bliss and heartbreak he rails without hatred against hypocrisy, corruption, and bad religion, he consorts free of lust with prostitutes and musicians. His awakening outshines the small idols of reason, emotion, self, desire, doctrine, even of Buddhism itself.

We translate Ikkyū because we love that shine, which is his mind. It is unbound, uncorrupt, effulgent, playful, and recondite. We hope to transmit something of its quality to an English-reading audience.

We don't know much about the human being we call Ikkyū. *The Chronology of the Monk Ikkyū of the Eastern Sea*, written by a disciple, gives only a year-by-year outline of Ikkyū's public life. It tells us that he was the son of a seventeen-year-old Emperor by a palace concubine, born auspiciously on New Year's Day 1394—the first of February by the Gregorian calendar. If this is so, then the story is at once political: one hundred years previous, an Emperor had rebelled against his generals, establishing an exile Southern Court in opposition to their Northern Court in Kyōtō. The split was only repaired a century after Ikkyū's death by the reunification of Japan under the Tokugawa. Ikkyū lived through recurrent civil wars: periodic vast starvation, the burning of Kyōtō, and fragile armistices when both sides reached exhaustion. Ikkyū's mother is said to have been a Southern aristocrat, a peace offering; Northern jealousies saw a knife up both her sleeves. She and Ikkyū were thus soon banished to the Long Gate Palace, seat of disfavored concubines, and his imperial patrimony concealed.

At age five, Ikkyū went alone into a minor Kyōtō monastery, where he received a good education—that is, he was trained in Buddhist doctrine and the high cultures of China. In particular, he learned to compose classical poetry in that language. (The poems we translate here are all of that genre.) Zen monasteries of the period functioned in ways reminiscent of the medieval European church. They were lavishly patronized, rich in land and peasant farmers, traders in luxury goods, repositories of culture and its accoutrements, and perfectly interpenetrated by the concerns of their political lords. These make a poor home for serious Zen practice, and Ikkyū's home temple Daitoku-ji was no exception. At sixteen years old, he quit in disgust and for the next fifteen years trained in poverty under the two most exacting Zen masters he could find. In the end both masters were dead, and he had attained his first enlightenments and the name Ikkyū 一休, meaning "Having Once Paused."

For the next fifty years he lived in and around Kyōtō and Sakai, a suburb of modern Ōsaka whose merchant and artistic cultures parallel Renaissance Venice. He remained an outsider to established religion, ever disgusted by its cant and compromise. "I'm just as likely to be found in a brothel as a temple," he wrote. Though we know him best through his poetry, he also collaborated intensively with artists who were reworking the whole of the medieval aesthetic. His influence shaped their calligraphy, Noh theater, linked verse, tea ceremony, and rock gardening, all of which now define Japan's sense of its cultural tradition.

In this book we translate some fifty poems, divided into four slightly overlapping sections. The first consists of poems dedicated to Zen masters of China and Japan, lineage founders who preceded Ikkyū and whose tradition lives in him. The great Linji, whom Japanese call Rinzai, is prominent among them, but a dozen more sublime masters also appear.

Second is a set of poems containing the term *fūryū* 風流. It's a two-syllable word: "fū" is pronounced "foo," and "ryū" is pronounced like the English word "cue," but with an r in the place of the c. Its literal meaning is "the flow of wind," but it holds within itself a grand expanse of human exploration. In a China some thousand years before Ikkyū, it was a style of elegant sensuality. Soon, though, its elegance emerged as the refinements of eremitic joy and simple beauty. Japan played out both its gaudiness and restraint. Ikkyū upholds all these usages and then subsumes them under a higher one: fūryū is his heart-broken appreciation for the play of appearance, for mystery. It's the center of his aesthetic, and he shows it differently in each poem. We have therefore left it untranslated. The subsequent essay, by Traktung Yeshe Dorje, expands on the term.

Third is a set of nine poems that Ikkyū wrote on the night of 18 October 1447. They are among his few writings we can date with certainty. Daitoku-ji had been nearly alone among Buddhist establishments in retaining the right to appoint its abbot from within, thus controlling the intrusion of political powers. When this privilege was rescinded on a technicality, the monks rioted. Ikkyū, in turn, walked out of Kyōtō and began a hunger strike, recorded in this poem cycle.

Finally there are a dozen poems to his lover Mori. They met when he was in his seventies, she a blind musician in her thirties or forties. They lived together until Ikkyū's death eleven years later. We know her almost exclusively through his poetry. She appears there only as "Mori," which is her surname, or as "the attendant Mori," or simply as "the blind woman."

A thousand of Ikkyū's poems are gathered in the *Crazy Cloud Collection* and its addenda. It's not unusual that he wrote in classical Chinese—it was the language in which Buddhism had come to Japan, and many important texts, religious or otherwise, continued to be written in it. His chief model was the four-line Regulated Verse of Tang China, a poem-form with five or seven words per line. Rhyme, rhythm, tonal pattern, and parallelism are all prescribed; diction and subject-matter are also controlled. All well-educated people wrote such poetry, with results varying from the inspired to the very ordinary. Another model for Ikkyū was the Sanskrit-derived *gatha*, short poems attesting to one's awakening. The first poem we translate in this book is the gatha Ikkyū wrote for his teacher Kasō, when he was enlightened at age twenty-six.

The Buddhist practitioner has been called a lotus, growing pure and fragrant from the muck of a swamp. But in these poems Ikkyū is swamp and lotus both: he cannot be sullied by circumstance, by birth and death, by identity, by either impurity or purity. His ongoing moment of enlightenment changes how this world appears. If we are deluded, we see mostly its degrading forces. But in unborn wisdom mind, "the great one-thousand worlds manifest from primordial purity," writes Ikkyū. Thus, "When I enter a brothel, I display this same great wisdom."

It's easy to get the wrong idea about Ikkyū's rage against corruption and his love of women. He may look Bohemian, yet there's no trace in him of self-indulgence. He seems rebellious, but his refusals are so profound that they sweep away even the category "rebel." He might be called antinomian save for an utter fidelity to the deep conventions of his practice lineage. He's been compared to the eccentric monk-poets Nankō Sōgan and Banri Shūkyū, his near contemporaries, but Ikkyū's supposed eccentricity is only the surface of a deeper mystery. It may also be shocking to know that at age eighty he became abbot of Daitoku-ji, his erstwhile home temple and brunt of his most vitriolic attacks. Its rebuilding from the ruination of civil war was launched under his tutelage.

Ikkyū's poetry is also unpredictable. He may argue out the most delicate of doctrinal matters and then plunge us raw into grief and outrage. His intimacy, with himself and with the reader, is unprecedented. His language, often the rough colloquial of Song dynasty Zen, shows an indifference to poetic convention, though never from a lack of skill. His juxtapositions are shocking and unexplained, sometimes even puzzling to his modern Japanese editors.

It is common in Tang-style poetry to sample previous verse or prose work. Thus two words, like "cloud-rain," conjure up the story of the King of Chu and his shaman lover, who shared one night of passion and never met again. Ikkyū goes much further than most poets, pulling frequent allusions out of the full range of China's cultural history and literature. He draws as well from a wide variety of Buddhist texts in Chinese, including its kōans. He never explains these allusions, simply assuming a readership as well educated as he. Translators have generally chosen one of two solutions to this richness: some have expanded Ikkyū's line to include as much information as possible, while others have added extensive annotations.

For this project we developed a new approach. We wondered, what would fourteenth-century readers bring with them to Ikkyū's work? How could we reproduce that knowledge for a twenty-first-century audience? Our solution was to write a brief lyric essay to introduce each poem, identifying Ikkyū's otherwise invisible inter-locutors through a mixture of story, translation, history, and lore. These essays are more assemblages than narrative, one piece placed beside another until they create a cloud of knowledge. However, ma-terials we have translated are always marked as such. Those who read Chinese or Japanese can find their sources in brief notes at the end of this book.

The same ancient story may be retold in multiple ways. For ex-ample, the King of Chu and his consort wander through these poem-worlds, each version showing another face of their relationship. The two wives of Sage Emperor Shun are sometimes paragons of grief and elsewhere slaves of their sexual desire. The sinking moon may in one instance recall the poetry of a desolate frontier and in another the story of imperial demise.

Allusion may also be understood as a mode of reincarnation. A phrase, figure, place takes new life in new surroundings. The Long Gate Palace, where Ikkyū's mother was exiled in the first poem we translate, is the Zhaoyang Palace of Han Dynasty China, a thousand miles and years away. Its inhabitants have different names and bod-ies, but they tell the same story. A Tang Emperor and his fabled con-sort become Ikkyū and Mori, who also take the "three-lives vow" to be reborn together in past, present, and future times. Ikkyū regarded himself as the incarnation of the Chinese Master Xutang, seven gen-erations previous, whose Japanese student brought his Rinzai lineage to fruit as Daitoku-ji. Two conjoint portraits survive with Xutang's beard on Ikkyū's face.

In a broader sense, Ikkyū's closest kin are those who devote themselves so completely to God or Love or Emptiness that all ref-erence points become irrelevant. Daitō, the founder of Daitoku-ji, spent seven years after his enlightenment living as a beggar under Kyōto's Fifth Street Bridge. That tradition lives today, as in the late twentieth-century figures Jung Kwang, a Korean monk-painter who practiced "unlimited action," and Franklin Jones (Adi Da) and Chō-gyam Trungpa, masters of "crazy wisdom." Like them, Ikkyū allowed a ceaseless compassion to burn his spirit so deeply that only an unadorned boldness remained.

Our work has been preceded by the labors of many. Donald Keene was the first to publish Ikkyū's poetry in English. Inspired by this, James Sanford wrote a pioneering study of his life and translation of his work. Jon Carter Covell gathered poems from Ikkyū's temples that had not been included in the standard collections. Already Sonja Arntzen had been working on a project that culminated in her excellent book on Ikkyū and the *Crazy Cloud Anthology*. A more recent article by Peipei Qiu explicates the history of fūryū. Full citations are available in the notes at the end of this book.

To accomplish our translation we have used the elegantly definitive five-volume collection of Ikkyū's writings and calligraphy edited by Hirano Sōjō 平野宗淨 and his colleagues, *Ikkyū Oshō zenshū* 一休和尚全集 (Tōkyō: Shunshūsha 春秋社, 1997). This includes the *Crazy Cloud Collection, The Chronology of the Monk Ikkyū of the Eastern Sea,* "Skeletons," and other writings. The *Crazy Cloud Collection* consists of 881 poems with strong attestation to Ikkyū. Our translations follow this numbering. Hirano et al. also include an appendix of 158 poems attributed to Ikkyū. The number "A122" indicates a poem from that addendum.

All Ikkyū students are in Hirano's debt. His unexcelled erudition has identified great numbers of Ikkyū's references. As well, most texts of Chinese and Japanese Buddhism have now become available in searchable digital format. This has made it possible to identify further allusions and connections, even for amateurs like us.

We use macrons in Japanese words but no diacritical marks for Sanskrit or other languages. The section "Notes and References" indicates the source for materials translated in our introduction to each poem. Rather than providing a full bibliographic reference, we've given sufficient information for a reader of Chinese or Japanese to identify and find the text in question.

We would like to thank the many friends who have assisted this work, especially Douglas Penick and Suzanne Wise. Quentin Crisp of Chomu Press (London) leant us his acute ears and eyes. Two anonymous readers for the University of Michigan Press provided essential guidance for our revisions. Heartfelt thanks to Aaron McCollough of the University of Michigan Press for seeing this project as a book when we were only at the edge of the nest. We are also thankful for institutional support from the University of North Carolina-Wilmington, the Radcliffe Institute for Advanced Study, and One Pause Poetry. Our inadequacy to this task will be apparent. We ask forgiveness of the lineage.

A Note on the Word Fūryū, Translation, and the Art of Magic

Translation is not a matter of words only: it is a matter of making intelligible a whole culture.
—Anthony Burgess

Making marks, talismans, amulets, words, paintings on the cave walls at Altamira—the mysterious magic and transformative power of communication. Languaging is the first and most primal magical act. The geographical landscape of language's activity, and the territory of magic, are one and the same. Like a river and its banks, language is shaped by and shapes consciousness in a self-structuring autopoiesis. It is for this reason that some words simply cannot, should not, be translated. To translate them is to bring them into our world by describing a limiting circle around their magical intentionality.

To translate Ikkyū's use of fūryū is to translate not only the whole culture but also the territory of Ikkyū's magical enlightened perception. Perhaps it is best to allow Ikkyū to translate us into his world rather than us translate his world into ours. Wind flow, impermanence, elegance, a sensual liberation theology of aesthetics, the tender heartbreak of nonjudgment, the silence and beauty of nature, a sophisticated tempest—all of these are fūryū, and more. Ikkyū says, "The guys down at the brothel, these too are fūryū." In his time those guys were akin to Williamsburg hipsters at an oxygen bar. To see these shallow dandies with the nonjudgmental openness of great compassion is to arrive at an unexpected beauty. Ikkyū invites us into the singularity of springtime and fall in his perceptual magic.

Fūryū, for Ikkyū, is to see the world through the eyes of unborn wisdom mind. A mind that is utterly free and yet does not have the slightest trace of withdrawal from the sense fields' divulgence of wonderment. This meaning is not static but shifting within each context. The translators of these lovely works of magic have chosen to not translate the word fūryū. We have no equivalent. Our culture is lacking this particular magical maneuver. And our culture sorely needs to discover it. When tantric sadhanas are translated into new languages, the gnosemic power of mantras are left in the magical script of Sanskrit. Their meaning is to be found in the practice. In the same way fūryū is left in its own magical script, and the practice that finds its meaning is the alchemical act of entering into another's world through deciphering the magical diagrams called language.

In the western tradition a textbook of magic is called a grimoire. Ikkyū's poems are a grimoire. The word fūryū is a magical diagram whose meaning wishes to reveal itself to you as a sentiment, a flavor of feeling, imparted through the spells, here called poems. To understand Ikkyū's use of the magical word you will have to enter into Ikkyū's dimension of magical realism. Lucky is the one who takes the trouble to accomplish this alchemical feat.

—Traktung Yeshe Dorje

Written on Captiva Island, Florida, as the dawn rays of the sun broke the horizon. April 4, 2013, parinirvana of that consummate magician Chögyam Trungpa Rinpoche.

I.
Lineage

face-to-face with a portrait of Linji

Between black sky and black earth, inside the summer wind, a crow. "If you pass through this gate," says a sutra, "you're an *arhat* emerging from the dust," a monk whose small enlightenment has forsaken the Three Poisons of lust, anger, and indifference.

The indifferent crow lifts its body in air and glides like a concubine's dropped fan. Fifteen hundred years ago in China, two sisters stole the Emperor's heart with their cold, crow-black hair, and Lady Ban became a palace serving maid, a white silk fan abandoned on a shelf. Five hundred years later a poet remembered it:

> She holds the broom respectfully as the golden halls open at
>   first light.
> Taking the rounded palace fan, she paces here and there with
>   folded hands.
> Her white jade face cannot match the sensual colors of cold
>   crow,
> And still she tends the Zhaoyang Palace in the play of spotted
>   sunlight.

The palace of rejected concubines. Like Ikkyū's mother, removed to Long Gate Palace when politics changed.

The Chronology of the Monk Ikkyū of the Eastern Sea gives this account:

> Ikkyū was twenty six. One summer night he heard a crow and had understanding. He immediately brought his insight to Kasō, who said, "That is the realm of an arhat, not a master." Ikkyū said, "I only like arhats. I detest masters." So Kasō said, "You are a true master."

It was the night of the 30th of June 1420. Kasō wanted a gatha to record it, so Ikkyū wrote:

Enlightenment

Ten years ago I couldn't stop thinking, feeling,
Just anger, just rage, until this moment.
A crow laughs, the dust clears, I hold the arhat's fruit.
Spotted sunlight in the Zhaoyang Palace, a pale face chanting.

十年以前識情心
嗔恚豪氣在即今
鴉咲出塵羅漢果
昭陽日影玉顏吟

In his youth, Linji lived as such a pure monk, in complete accordance with the Vinaya, Buddha's monastic rule, that only Huangbo's stick could smack him loose.

Two hundred fifty years later in Linji's lineage arose the great monk Yuanwu, so assiduous in his practice that he was called Diligence. His story goes like this:

> Diligence's teacher addressed a lay visitor, saying "When you were young, perhaps you read the love poem by Emperor Wu? The last two lines are very close to the meaning of why Bodhidharma came from the west. They read,
>
>> Oh, oh, these small bits of jade mean nothing.
>> I only want to hear the sounds of my lover."
>
> Just then Diligence came in, heard this, and making a doubtful face, asked, "Has he mastered it?"
>
> The teacher replied, "He has only attained the sound."
>
> "Since he knows the sound, then why can't he see the dao?"
>
> His teacher yelled an old kōan question-and-response, "What is the meaning of why Bodhidharma came from the west? The cypress tree in front of the garden!"
>
> Diligence was instantly enlightened. Bounding out of the room, he saw a cock fly to the top of the railing, beat its wings and crow loudly. He laughed and said, "Isn't this the sound of 'I only want to hear the sounds of my lover'?" Then he wrote a gatha expressing his enlightenment and presented it to his teacher. It said,
>
>> The fūryū affair of her youth
>> Can only be known by the beauty herself.
>
> His teacher said to him, "Today your sounds are joined with those of all the Buddhas."

Praising the Monk Linji

All along Dao's work: just monastic rules.
Huangbo's stick meets head . . . . . . great unknowing.
Transmission, clear and true, Diligence's bulls-eye.
Chanting that fūryū love poem until it's completely broken
    open.

贊臨濟和尚

從來道業是毘尼
黃檗棒頭忘所知
正傳的的克勤下
吟破風流小豔詩

Where do Linji's heart teachings lie? Is it in the Three Mysteries and Three Essentials that everyone called his true dharma eye? But he never explained what those were.

As Linji was dying, he gathered monks in the assembly hall, saying, "After I am extinguished, don't extinguish my true dharma eye."

Sansheng burst out, "How would I dare extinguish your true dharma eye?"

Linji said, "Afterwards, if people ask you, what will you say?"

Sansheng just shouted.

Linji said, "Who'd have known that my true dharma eye would come to extinction right here in front of this blind donkey."

He finished speaking. Then, sitting upright, he died.

And a master adds, "The Blind Donkey Sansheng is a true son of Linji."

Once Ikkyū lived in a shack he called "Hut of the Blind Donkey." Later he named himself "Dream Boudoir," saying:

If you are thirsty in the dream, you dream of water. If you are cold in it, you dream of a fur coat. To dream of the boudoir—that's my nature. I've lately taken the name "Dream Boudoir" and set it on a plaque above my studio. I'm just a crazy old scoundrel, advertising what I like.

Face-to-face with a Portrait of Linji

Who in Linji's lineage dwells as true transmission?
Three mysteries, three essentials, a blind donkey.
This old monk Dream Boudoir, a moon inside the boudoir.
Night after night, fūryū, right here in front of this sodden
    drunk.

對臨濟畫像

臨濟宗門誰正傳
三玄三要瞎驢邊
夢閨老衲閨中月
夜夜風流爛醉前

"Pine window, the moon reflects my idleness," writes a Tang poet. And another adds:

In the evening I sit beneath the old green pine.
At night I sleep inside the bamboo pavilion.

A thousand years before, the King of Chu climbed Cloud Dream terrace, where he met the goddess of Shaman Mountain. She said to him, "I wish to serve at your pillow and sleeping mat." The next morning she became the mist of the high peaks and disappeared. Since then, their night together has been called "cloud dreams and idle feelings."

One day while Linji was planting pines, Huangbo asked him, "What are you doing, planting all these trees deep in the mountains?"

Linji said, "For one, this offering will improve the environment around our monastery's Mountain Gate. For another, this offering will persist and impress future generations." Having spoken, he took his mattock and hit the ground three times.

Huangbo said, "Even so, I've already beaten you some thirty times."

Linji again took his mattock and hit the ground three times, making a "shu shu" sound. Huangbo said, "Now that my lineage has reached you, it will flourish greatly in the world."

Pine Window
a name for my studio

Thatched cottages and bamboo pavilions—no one can stop
   this flourishing.
Linji comes planting, and it's not empty work.
Here on my pillow, I'm ashamed of my idle dreams.
Night comes, I rise startled: wind from the latrine.

松窗
   齋名

茅廬竹閣興難窮
臨濟栽來功不空
枕上自慚有閑夢
夜來驚起屋頭風

Buddha enumerated five heinous crimes: to kill mother, father, a monastic, to shed a Buddha's blood, to split the community. Anyone committing such crimes creates the karma to be born in the Avici hell, the eighth of the eight hot hells, called in Chinese "no-space hell."

Linji said:

Mind is born, and every sort of dharma is born.
Mind is extinguished, and every sort of dharma is extinguished.
When one mind is unborn, ten-thousand dharmas are without fault.
In this world and beyond this world, there is no buddha, no dharma, nor is anything present, nor was anything lost. Names and phrases are not of themselves names and phrases. It's only you in the present, radiant and bright, perceiving, understanding, and illuminating, who attach all names and phrases.
Great virtuous ones, it is just by creating the five no-space karmas that you attain emancipation.

How are these five crimes liberation? A student asked Master Wuzu, "How are things in the lineage after Linji?" and he replied "Five crimes and hearing thunder." People took this to mean that if you commit one of the five crimes, you'll hear thunder, because lighting's about to strike your head. But by "five crimes" Wuzu meant the shouts and beatings, the overturning of monks, appropriate and inappropriate, Linji's wild acts of liberation.

The *Vimalakirti Sutra* says, "When the bodhisattva practices the five no-space crimes without lust or hatred, he enters the various hells without the filth of sin." To kill, to destroy without lust or hatred, to love beings with perfect kindness, beyond crimes and beyond no-crimes, this is liberation.

The Precept Against Praising Oneself and Destroying Others

"Five crimes and hearing thunder," Linji's tricks of the trade.
His great love and great compassion are so very kind.
The sword that gives life, the knife that kills.
If you're planning to defile someone, your mouth will fill with
    blood.

自讚毀他戒

五逆聞雷臨濟訣
大慈大悲太親切
活人劍兮殺人刀
欲污人滿口含血

The *Record of Linji* states:

When Linji was first in Huangbo's assembly, his conduct was simple and pure. The head monk thus praised him, saying, "Though just a lad, he's different from the others."

And then he became the great master Linji. Such masters are "a sword so long that it leans against the sky," says an ancient text, "stern and awesome, in full majesty." And it adds: "If someone rides a tiger's head, he must have a sword in his hand."

The *Record of Linji* continues:

A monk asked, "What about 'take away the environment, not take away the person'?"
　　Linji said:

　　　　The king's orders already pervade the realm.
　　　　The general settles the dust beyond the borders.

Ikkyū dreamed he met a skeleton in a field. He asked himself:

So what moment is not a dream? What person won't be a skeleton? We operate as skeletons wrapped in five-colored skin, so there is the sexual desire of male and female. When breath is cut off and the skin bursts open, there is no sexual desire.

An old saying: "Buddha-nature shows its magnificence, but sentient beings who dwell in appearances have difficulty seeing it."

poem # 615

Praising Myself

My long sword glows as it leans against heaven,
My skeleton displays its magnificence—
Such singular fame this pure general.
But at my core, fūryū and love of sex.

自賛

倚天長劍光
骨骼露堂堂
純一將軍譽
風流好色腸

Two stories. The first is about the monk who heard a woman singing from the pavilion, and this was enough.

One day he happened to be walking through the streets, and he stopped to adjust his legging straps in front of a wine pavilion. He heard someone upstairs singing, "Since you are heartless already, I too will stop."

But the Chinese word "heartless" can also be heard as "mindless," meaning Zen-emptiness. As in, since you are already mindless, I too will stop.

Suddenly he was greatly enlightened, and because of that he was called "Pavilion."

The name Ikkyū also means "Once Stopped."

The second story is about the Zen teacher Ciming, who was hard to find. He didn't show up for dharma talks and skipped his private audiences with the monks. One desperate student followed him as he left the monastery. Ciming was going to his lover's house—the student saw them cooking together in the kitchen, and blushed.

Idle Meditation Defiles the Gaudy, Braggart Student

The gold-robed elders' life-long desire
Is to gather the assembly, practice Zen, and give lectures from
    the dais.
What are the strategies of Pavilion Monk and Ciming?
The face-paint of a lovely, fūryū beauty.

閑工夫辱榮衒徒

金襴長老一生望
集眾參禪又上堂
樓子慈明何作略
風流可愛美人粧

The Buddha held up a silent flower, and among the whole assembly only Kasyapa smiled. Thus he became the first patriarch of Zen. Perhaps he went next to southern China, a thousand years before Bodhidharma, settling on Chicken Foot Mountain. There he will practice meditation for millions and billions of years, until the next Buddha is born.

Yang Guifei, consort of the Tang Emperor, was one of the Four Beauties of ancient China—the Emperor loved her beyond all else, hiring seven hundred laborers to sew fabric for her gowns. Years of spring love-making, and then disaster, rebellion rending all China. His soldiers blamed it on her dalliance in politics and demanded her death. The Emperor had an impossible choice. She was strangled at Mawei Mountain. After that, they saw each other only in dreams, where they renewed their vow to be born together as husband and wife in the three lives, past, present, and future.

The ancient sage Zhuangzi knew the unturning pivot at the center of all activity. He said, "When 'this' and 'that' do not find their mate, it's called the pivot of the dao. When the pivot finally finds its central point, it can respond endlessly. Its right is a single endlessness, and its wrong is a single endlessness."

The Twenty-Second Patriarch of Zen said it like this:

The mind revolves, following the ten thousand realms,
Its power hidden in the pivot-point.
Follow the flow until you recognize its true nature.
Then you are without both happiness and distress.

Yet Linji's Zen practices all happiness and all distress, together for the three lives.

Correct Meditation Reveals the Long-Practicing Student

The power hidden in a wheel's pivot-point:
Both Linji's true transmission, and schemes for fame and
　　wealth.
One pillow, spring wind, dawn at Chicken Foot Mountain.
Three lives, night wine, autumn at Mawei.

正工夫示久參徒

機輪轉處實能幽
臨濟正傳名利謀
一枕春風雞足曉
三生夜酒馬嵬秋

From an old Chinese cautionary tale: don't straighten your hat when you're standing under a pear tree, people will think you're stealing fruit. A Song poet writes:

> Brothel and wineshop, the idle lay Buddhist,
> How could a pear tree keep him from straightening his hat?

Meanwhile, the Pavilion Monk writes of the match-maker's red thread that ties one to the beloved:

> Night lodging: flower city and wine pavilion.
> Once I'd heard the song and flute, sadness seemed left
>   behind.
> A sharp knife pulls and snaps the red thread.
> If you're without a heart or mind, then I'll just stop.

Love's longing, the depth of passion, is held just for a moment in cloud and rain.

Ode to the Brothel

Beautiful woman, cloud and rain, love's deep river.
Old Zen Pavilion Monk, up in the pavilion singing.
I have such refined passion for hugging and kissing.
My mind doesn't say: the world is a fire, give up your body.

題婬坊

美人雲雨愛河深
樓子老禪樓上吟
我有抱持嚏吻興
意無火聚捨身心

The Chinese master Xutang, who began the lineage of Daitoku-ji, had three turning phrases meant to jolt the mind from ignorance into awakening.

As a youth, Master Dengzhou was always looking for the right phrase, but he never found it. "Speak, speak," said the head monk. Dengzhou couldn't respond. When he finally offered a few words, the monk said they were all wrong.

Dengzhou asked, "Will you please say it for me, then?"

The monk replied, "What I say would be my own understanding. How would that be of benefit to you?"

Dengzhou returned to the dormitory. He went through all the phrases he had collected, but there wasn't a single word with which he could reply to the monk. He sighed to himself saying, "If you paint a picture of a cake, it can't ease your hunger." So he burned all his books and said, "In this lifetime I will never realize the Buddha-dharma." Then, weeping, he bade farewell to his teacher and left.

Linji's monks were always looking for the right understanding, but they never found it. Addressing the monks, he said:

If you have ceaseless thoughts, and your mind never rests, this is climbing up the tree of non-enlightenment. You'll be born in one of the six realms, with fur on your body and horns on your head.

When not a single thought is born, this is climbing up the tree of Buddha's enlightenment. Then dharma's a pleasure and Zen a delight. If you think of clothing, a thousand silk garments appear. If you think of food, you'll be sated by a feast of a hundred flavors.

Enlightenment dwells nowhere. Therefore there is no one who attains it.

The Three Turning Phrases of the Monk Xutang (poem one)
Your eyes are not yet opened,
so how could you make
pants for Xutang?

When you're freezing and hungry, paintings of cakes won't
satisfy.

The eyes you are born with see like a blind man.

At night in the cold hall: think of clothing,

And a thousand silk garments will miraculously appear.

虛堂和尚三轉語
己眼未明底
因甚將虛堂
作布袴着

畫餅冷腸飢未盛

娘生己眼見如盲

寒堂一夜思衣意

羅綺千重暗現成

Buddha gave everyone a gift that has no value and no price. A Chinese master wrote:

The spirit radiance shines of itself,
Its full manifestation true and constant.
It cannot be captured by words and letters.
This is perfect buddhahood.

The buddha-lineage of Xutang was brought to Japan by the work of ceaseless meditation and carried onward by Daitō, founder of Daitoku-ji. In his own hand the Emperor wrote "Spirit Radiance" on Daitō's tomb.

How do we repay the Buddha's gift? A Zen patriarch replied:

At the Surangama assembly, Ananda praised the Buddha, saying, "With my whole heart and mind I will revere the infinity of appearances." This is called "repaying the Buddha's blessing."

In the port city of Sakai one could buy or sell temples, kōans, certificates, or sermons. And so the Chinese warning against being taken for a thief: "Don't tie your shoes in a melon patch, don't straighten your hat under a pear tree." But the purity of a true master—his interventions, manipulations, and strategies—is indifferent to gossip, is only a perfect response to the needs of beings.

Severing Relations with the Sakai Crowd

Xutang's grandchildren are addicted to wealth and in love
    with fame.
The spirit radiance of Daitō's lineage has been completely
    lost.
Pear hats and melon shoes—people get suspicious.
But skill repays the Buddha's blessing with its perfect tricks.

泉堺眾絕交

耽利好名天澤孫
靈光失卻大燈門
梨冠瓜履人疑念
伎倆當機報佛恩

The King of Chu, dreaming of his spirit consort, asks, "Who are you?" She replies, "In the morning I am the clouds, in the evening I am the rain. We will not meet again in these bodies."

A thousand years later, four men and women, praising the moon and wine, write a poem, one line each. Each line must contain the word "moon" and "goblet." If they hesitate, they have to drink three cups of wine as penalty:

> The father says:
>> The single-wheel bright moon shines on the golden goblet.
> The son:
>> Wine fills the golden goblet, moon fills the wheel.
> The daughter:
>> The bright moon hangs upside down inside the golden
>> goblet.
> The son-in-law:
>> I raise up the wine goblet and swallow down the moon.

A Zen contemporary of theirs writes:

> The Son of Heaven of the sacred court sits in the Bright Hall.
> Beings and spirits within the four seas pillow their heads in
>> utter peace.
> Youthful fūryū turns the golden goblet upside down.
> Peach blossoms fill the courtyard like red brocade.

"Where is the mountain demon cave?" asks another Zen master. "It's that place in a large monastic gathering where the Way dwells without going or dwelling. So smash it. Chatting like this is precisely the demon cave."

Crazy Cloud truly is Daitō's grandson.
What's honorable about demon caves and black mountains?
I think of the past. Flute songs, evenings of cloud and rain.
Youthful fūryū turns the golden goblet upside down.

狂雲真是大燈孫
鬼窟黑山何稱尊
憶昔簫歌雲雨夕
風流年少倒金樽

Daitō's name means "Great Lamp." In 1326 he founded Daitoku-ji. In August 1453, most of it burned to the ground. Linji used to say, "Sometimes I take away both the person and the environment."

And yet always the Buddha's body, the Buddha's speech, the Buddha's mind. Linji called these the Three Mysteries, naming the first "the mystery within the body." Huineng, the Sixth Patriarch, said, "All of you people, your own mind is the Buddha!" Ikkyū wrote: "'Take away the person, take away the environment'—this is the mystery within the body."

The Chronology of the Monk Ikkyū of the Eastern Sea tells of the Daitoku-ji fire:

August. The towering heat and smoke of the conflagration. The bell and wooden fish, used to mark practice, were silent. Only the bathhouse, the veranda to the main gate, the Nyoi-an and the Daiyō-an remained. Then the monk Yōsō tore down the Daiyō-an to build the Spirit Radiance Pagoda to Daitō. Ikkyū wrote this gatha regarding the pagoda:

Regarding the Pagoda of National Teacher Daitō, After the
Daitoku-ji Fire

Drafted 128 years ago,
Today it looks like a dark mystery within the body.
After orthodoxy and heterodoxy, environment and dharma,
    have been completely destroyed,
There's still that Great Lamp, radiating through the great
    1000 worlds.

大德寺火後題大燈國師塔

創草百二十八年
看來今日體中玄
正邪境法滅卻後
猶是大燈輝大千

Pious worshippers scatter powdered incense on statues of the Buddha to increase their miraculous power.

"Your childish prattle gives me a sour face," goes a poem from Southern Song.

poem #454

I Hate Incense

Who can even discuss a master's methods?
Speaking of Dao, talking of Zen, your tongues grow long.
Old Ikkyū abhors your scrambling after marvels.
I make a pinched, sour face, all this incense thrown on the
　　Buddha.

嫌抹香

作家手段孰商量
說道談禪舌更長
純老天然惡殊勝
暗顰鼻孔佛前香

The *Blue Cliff Record* sets out this kōan:

> One day Yanguan called to his attendant, "Bring me the rhinoceros fan."
>
> The attendant said, "The fan is broken."
>
> Yanguan said, "Since the fan is broken, then give me back the rhinoceros itself."
>
> The attendant had no reply.

That precious horn of Buddha-nature that grows on the head of every sentient being—where is it now, and how will we ever get it back?

Vagrant Lu wandered into the temple of the Fifth Patriarch.

> The Patriarch asked him, "Who are you and what do you want?"
>
> He said, "I'm a southerner, and I want to become a Buddha."
>
> "Southerners don't have Buddha-nature."
>
> "Men are southern and northern, but Buddha-nature has no south and north."

And so Lu became a student of the Fifth Patriarch and eventually turned into Huineng, the Great Sixth Patriarch of Chinese Zen.

Who is given the rhinoceros-horn fan?
And what if Lord Lu wanders in the door?
Constant talk of famous families in the dharma hall,
As if in the office of a hundred imperial bureaucrats.

犀牛扇子與誰人
行者盧公來作賓
姓名議論法堂上
恰似百官朝紫宸

Puhua, eating raw vegetables outside the meditation hall or tip-
ping over the dinner table—the only one who ever got the better of
Linji. He'd scourge the streets, tugging and overturning everything.
He'd say:

> When brightness comes, hitting brightness.
> When darkness comes, hitting darkness.
> When the four directions and eight sides come, a whirlwind
>   hits.
> When emptiness comes, I hit like a flail.

Or the time a monk asked Zhaozhou, "What is Zhaozhou?" and he
said, "East gate, west gate, south gate, north gate."

In *The Chronology of The Monk Ikkyū of the Eastern Sea* it states:

> Someone asked Kasō, "After your death, to whom will your
> dharma be transmitted?"
>
> He replied, "Although his way is crazy, there's this pure
> young guy, Ikkyū."

Praising Myself

Crazy, crazy man roils up a crazy wind,
Coming and going between brothels and wine shops.
Is there an un-blind monk who can test my understanding?
Painting south, painting north, painting west and east.

自贊

風狂狂客起狂風
來往婬坊酒肆中
具眼衲僧誰一拶
畫南畫北畫西東

II.
Fūryū

---

the flow of wind

The monk Lingyun practiced Zen for thirty years without any understanding. By chance one day he saw a peach tree, luxuriant and in full bloom. Suddenly he was enlightened, and his joy was beyond all understanding. A poem says:

> At root there is no delusion or enlightenment, a jumble
>   beyond enumeration.
> Lingyun alone is a true master.
> May I ask all honored patriarchs everywhere
> If they know the spot to see peach blossoms?

The Queen Mother of the West, she of Pure Jade Pond, lives in the distant Kunlun Mountains, where earth borders heaven. Golden peaches of immortality grow on her tree. At auspicious moments she has invited great emperors of China to join her and enjoy her peaches of eternal life. But none could hold his place beside her, so each remained merely human, dying in sorrow.

Upon Seeing a Picture of Peach Blossoms

Seeing the spot, fūryū enlightens the mind of dao.
One branch of peach blossoms is worth a thousand ounces of
    gold.
Queen Mother of Pure Jade Pond, face of spring wind.
I bind myself to the men of sorrow, songs of cloud and rain.

見桃花圖

見處風流悟道心
桃花一條價千金
瑤池王母春風面
我約愁人雲雨吟

Once there was a monk known only as Old Ding. He asked Linji, "What is the great meaning of Buddha's dharma?" Linji got down from his dais and slapped him. Ding just stood there, frozen. The monk sitting next to him said, "Ding, why don't you bow?" As Ding bowed, suddenly he was greatly enlightened.

Afterwards, he meets a couple of monks on the road. "Where're you coming from?" they ask. "Linji." "Give us something of him," they ask, so he tells the famous story of Linji, who said:

In this lump of raw red meat is a true man without rank.

And when someone asked Linji what that is, he'd say,

The true man without rank is just some dried shit-stick.

But the monks on the road with Ding can't grasp it. One's mouth falls open. The other asks, "Why don't you say 'Not a true man without rank'?"

Old Ding says, "A true man without rank and not a true man without rank, how far apart are they? Quickly, quickly, speak." But he couldn't answer. So Ding says, "If you guys weren't so old, I'd beat both you bed-wetting imps to death."

The bed-wetting imp is a man in great distress.
Old Ding has the right trick, the power of his blessings is
    deep.
Night rain. Before the lamp, confusion is already forgotten.
In the fūryū tea-house, chanting ancient times.

尿床鬼子大難心
定老當機恩力深
夜雨燈前渾即忘
風流茶店舊時吟

Shaman Mountain, the dream of the King of Chu, clouds and rain.

The *Blue Cliff Record* sets out this case:

Jingqing asked a monk, "What's that sound outside?"
The monk said, "The sound of rain drops."
Jingqing said, "Sentient beings are all topsy-turvy. They delude themselves pursuing things outside themselves."

So when Zhuangzi asks himself, "What is a gentleman of the rivers and seas?" he answers, "He moves in close to the marsh, dwells freely in bright vastness, and fishes in an idle spot, doing nothing at all."

In the realm of that vast brightness, the sages of highest antiquity discerned patterns in the natural world, pattern forces they called Qian and Kun. Qian and Kun are Heaven and Earth, are the active and the receptive, male and female, the first two hexagrams of the *Yijing* or *Book of Change*.

More than two thousand years afterwards, rebellion rends China. The Tang Emperor gives up his concubine Yang Guifei to be killed and abdicates the throne to his son. A verse:

The moon, sinking, sinking. . . .
The fūryū Emperor does not return.

During that rebellion, Du Fu, China's greatest poet, flees the capital with his family, securing them outside a farming village at Fuzhou. Then he travels out to serve the new Emperor. On the road he's captured by rebel troops and returned to the capital. From there he writes his wife:

When will we lean against the open screen,
The moon shining on us both, drying the traces of tears?

On Shaman Mountain rain drops join in a new song.
Lewd fūryū, my poetry is also lewd.
Rivers and seas, Qian and Kun, the tears of Du Fu.
In Fuzhou, tonight the moon is sinking, sinking.

巫山雨滴入新吟
婬色風流詩亦婬
江海乾坤杜陵淚
鄜州今夜月沈沈

Manjushri is the bodhisattva of wisdom. But what is that wisdom?

Buddha's great disciple Ananda accomplished the wisdom of an *arhat*, someone who has left the red dust of samsara behind, who is free of desire and hatred.

But a bodhisattva attains Manjushri's Great Wisdom and finally Buddhahood only by never abandoning the sorrows of samsara.

The *Lankavatara Sutra* tells this story:

> At that time Ananda went begging for food and, following along the streets, passed by some brothels. There he met the woman Matangi, who had great skill in sorcery and used the Kapila Brahma mantra to draw him inside. She bent forward, fondling him, and was about to destroy the essence of his vows.

The Buddha himself, dwelling in vast space, saw this delicate moment, and sent the bodhisattva Manjushri to recite a mantra that would counter her sorcery.

> The evil spell was extinguished. Thereupon Ananda and Matangi were carried off to the place of the Buddha. Ananda prostrated and put the Buddha's feet on his head, weeping in compassion.

An arhat emerges from dust and thus pushes Buddhahood
   away.
When I enter a brothel, I display Great Wisdom.
I laugh deeply at Manjushri reciting the *Lankavatara Sutra*.
He has lost the whole business of his youthful fūryū.

出塵羅漢遠佛地
一入婬坊發大智
深咲文殊唱楞經
失卻少年風流事

Thousands of years ago the Sage Emperor Shun ruled all China. Even though he was born into the poverty of a three-family village, wherever he went, he transformed society. Coming to a pottery-making village rife with quarrels, he brought such order that a year later their pots were more beautiful than ever. Coming to a fishing village rent by murderous squabbles, he brought peace. Learning of Shun's nobility, the Emperor Yao gave him his two daughters and the throne.

Because his wives had grown up spoiled by luxury, it is said that they were often filled with intemperate lust. With Shun, they learned to be humble and work the fields. Yet when he died, they forgot everything, and their unfulfilled passion drove them rushing to the spot where his body had fallen. They pleaded for his return, crying over his corpse until their tears turned to blood. The songs of their weeping might have brought down a dynasty, but Shun would not hear them.

Later, Confucius wrote:

> All vocal sounds arise from the human mind. The human mind responds to stimuli and moves, shaping itself in sound. Music is thus based in the human mind and its response to things.
>
> The way of sound is communicated through governance. If the five notes oppress each other, this is called "being out of tune." In that case, the state will soon come to its doom. The music in the Mulberry Grove above Pu River is the music of a doomed state.

poem #271

Pointing Out Lewd People

Singing salacious songs in the Mulberry Grove above Pu
   River,
And still my deepest reverence for youthful fūryū.
A traveler through the three-family villages of the world,
Shun did not recognize the songs of his two consorts.

示婬色人

濮上桑間唱哇音
風流年少寵尤深
世界三家村裏客
重華不識二妃吟

Zhuangzi was a true gentleman of the rivers and seas.

Master Yantou rowed his boat for two days across the lake, driven from his monastery in the religious persecution of late Tang.

Master Muzhou returned home to care for his mother, avoiding rebellion in the countryside. To support them both, he repaired straw sandals, using wild grape leaves he found along the road.

Linji said, "Sometimes I take away both the person and the environment."

Someone asked, "What is it when you don't take it away?"

He said, "The king ascends his jeweled hall, rustic elders sing their songs."

The practice of working the oars, Yantou's boat.

Muzhou weaves sandals, grape-leaf autumn.

Rustic elders can't hide their praise for straw hats and
raincoats.

What person? The rivers and seas, a single fūryū.

功夫勞棹谿公舟

尊宿織鞋蒲葉秋

野老難蔵蓑笠譽

誰人江海一風流

Four thousand years ago Emperor Shun's wives cried tears of blood over his body. Then they threw themselves into the River Xiang and drowned.

Two thousand years later the Marquis of Biyang was such a pet to the Han Empress that she made him Prime Minister, and anyone wanting access to her was dependent on his whim.

A thousand years after that, Li Qunyu encountered Shun's two wives as spirits of the River Xiang. They told him to meet them in two years, and they would all become lovers. A friend mocked him, "I didn't know you were the Biyang Marquis to Shun's two wives!" Li Qunyu wrote:

> For a moment we take up the wind and moon of sex,
>   resenting that the lake is calm.
> See completely how the water of the fusang tree is all dried
>   up.

"Fusang," which is what the Chinese call the nation of Japan. Li Qunyu's poem continues:

> The promises we made on the almond-blossom altar are
>   gone.
> Inside the painted game-box, we play at backgammon, red
>   and purple pieces.

Buddha gave laypeople five precepts. One prohibits improper sexual conduct, often interpreted as adultery, homosexuality, or masturbation. But Crazy Cloud Ikkyū writes about the sexual apparitions of suicide, politics, fantasy, and commerce.

The Precept Against Improper Sexual Conduct

The young people in the brothel are also fūryū.
They kiss and hug, the crazy guest is sad.
Deluded, Li Qunyu plays backgammon.
The great fame of Emperor Shun and the Biyang Marquis.

不邪淫戒

婬坊年少也風流
接吻抱持狂客愁
妄鬪樗蒲李群玉
名高虞舜辟陽侯

Gui Shan, meaning "Gui Mountain," is the name of a place and also the name of the monk presiding there, "Guishan." One day he gathered his disciples, saying:

> This old monk—a hundred years from now I'll go down the mountain to a patron's house and become a water-buffalo. On my left flank will be a line of five words, "I, a Gui Shan monk." At just this moment, calling it a Gui Shan monk is the same as calling it a water-buffalo.

That water-buffalo is always plowing, being eaten and used up in the Three Family Village, a place so destitute that even Zen masters make fun of it. Guishan took the bodhisattva vow to return again and again to live in this realm of suffering.

The *Sutra of Perfect Enlightenment* points to the perfect realization of every being. One class of its bodhisattvas is called "aware with their whole bodies," another "calm with their whole bodies."

poem #508

A Painting

Has Guishan really come back? Here's a buffalo,
Wearing horns, fur and a monk's head.
It's so sweet: different species, calm in one whole body.
Inside the Three Family Village is also fūryū.

畫

潙山來也目前牛
戴角披毛僧一頭
異類如甘一身靜
三家村裏也風流

An ancient tale:

Once there was a two-headed bird named Joint Fate who lived on Snow Mountain in the Himalayas. One head was tranquil and ate well, while the other was agitated and ate poorly. "Why does the other head always get good food, and I none?" the agitated head said, eating poisonous weeds.

Sometimes, when the bird flew off looking for food, it would forget its way back to the nest.

Both heads died at the same time.

Li Bo wrote a poem of desolation on the western frontier, "Moon cold, river clear, the night is sinking, sinking."

On a Cold Night, Sorrow for the Bird of Snow Mountain

Morning comes: kōan. Evening comes: repeating again and
    again.
Seeking food, always forgetting its nest—past karma's deep.
Day and night, everyone is the bird of Snow Mountain.
Suffering in the lowest hell, the moon is sinking, sinking.

寒夜嘆雪山鳥

朝來公案晚來吟
求食忘巢前業深
晝夜人人雪山鳥
無間苦痛月沈沈

Yang Guifei, glorious consort to the Tang Emperor. Delighting in their love-play, the Emperor left state affairs to her cousin, who corrupted government to enrich the Yang clan estates. Common people, soldiers and officials suffered from these entanglements. Their resentment led to rebellion, and that rebellion split the realm. Eight years later, half of China's population was lost to warfare and starvation. The poet Du Fu, "the loyal subject," his own son dying of malnutrition a thousand miles away, asked what might be the suffering of ordinary people if he, an official, knows such distress? In accord with imperial protocol, his poetry of remonstrance was addressed to the steps below the throne, rather than to the Emperor himself. Nonetheless it was always ignored.

Hino Tomiko, wife of the Ashikaga Shōgun, was determined to put her son in that seat ahead of anyone. Her feckless husband became the plaything of her clan, and as with Yang Guifei, her machinations divided the nation into two factions. Then ten years of the Ōnin War, blockades of rice shipments to the capital, the destruction of Daitoku-ji and all northern Kyōtō. Devastation throughout the nation of Fusang.

A Chinese master said, "The ongoing suffering of karma is always born from wealth and treasure."

poem #309

Respectfully Offered to the Steps Below the Son of Heaven

Wealth, treasure, rice and money create enemies of the court.
Fūryū lovers, don't think of each other!
Safety and danger are both bitter here in the nation of
    Fusang.
This loyal subject stands at the side with his heart of tangled
    threads.

敬上天子堦下

財寶米錢朝敵基
風流兒女莫相思
伏桑國裏安危苦
傍有忠臣心亂系

III.
Hunger

on the day of Double Nine

The following series of nine poems was written on the night of the ninth day of the ninth lunar month, 1447. For centuries Chinese and Japanese literati had taken the day of Double Nine to climb the hills outside of town, enjoy a picnic, and drink rice wine steeped in chrysanthemum blossoms. Instead, Ikkyū initiated a fast. For a hundred years his Daitoku-ji monstery had preserved the right to appoint their abbot exclusively from among the temple's monks. That autumn political authorities had placed an outsider over them. In response, a monk committed suicide—an extremely unusual form of protest. Abruptly, Ikkyū left Kyōtō for a small house he owned in the mountains thirty miles south.

The Chronology of the Monk Ikkyū of the Eastern Sea states:

Many incidents at Daitoku-ji, the Dragon Mountain—a number of monks were arrested and jailed. The whole temple was distressed. Autumn, the ninth month. Ikkyū was extremely heart-sick. Secretly, he entered the Yuzuriha Mountains, where he was going to starve himself to death.

The matter reached the Emperor's ears, so he sent down an imperial order saying, "If you are determined to carry out this plan, you will destroy both the Buddha's law of dharma and the royal law. How could you abandon us? How could you forget the nation?"

Ikkyū replied to the order, saying, "This poor man of dao is also a subject of Your Realm. How could he dare evade Your Command?"

In the fall of 1447, a monk at Daitoku-ji monastery killed himself for no good reason. In response, some gossiping monks made slanderous reports to the officials. Due to this misfortune, five or seven monks were imprisoned, bringing great chaos to our temple.

At that time, people spread many rumors. When I heard them, I immediately disappeared into the mountains. Maybe because I just couldn't bear it. A disciple from the capital chanced by and told me all the details. Hearing them, I was even more overcome with mourning and so wrote poetry to speak what was in my heart. Because it happened to be Double Yang, the ninth day of the ninth month, I wrote these nine pieces.

文安丁卯秋大德精舍有一僧無故而自殺矣
好事之徒遂譖之官繫其余殃而居囚禁者七
五輩足為吾門之大亂時人喧傳焉予聞之即
日晦跡山中其意蓋出於不忍耳適學者自京
城來說本寺件件之事愈弗勝慨嘆作偈言懷
時值重陽故成九篇云

1.

Disasters at Daitoku-ji, the Dragon Treasure temple. Two thousand years earlier Zhuangzi used to say:

> If it's an "is," then there will be an "isn't."
> If it's an "isn't," then there will be an "is."
> "Other" has its own "is/isn't," and "it" has its own "is/isn't."
> So are there really an other and an it?
> So are there really no other and no it?
> Thus the sage does not go by this way.

But still, disasters at Daitoku-ji. The temple founder, Daitō, tells this story:

> At the end of the summer training session, Cuiyan addressed the assembly. "All summer I've been talking for your benefit, brothers. Look, are Cuiyan's eyebrows still there?"

When a great criminal is about to enter hell, his eyebrows fall out. Cuiyan's offense: too much talking.

Zen students are all thieves, goes an old saying. So Master Baofu comments on Cuiyan's crime:

> You empty the thief's mind!

A later teacher adds:

> Then the thief can recognize his thievery.

Yunmen ended the whole conversation, by just shouting

> KAN!

"Kan," meaning the barrier, the gateless gate, the thought-stopper. Daitō said it even stops Baofu's thief when he's trying to escape.

Earth is old, heaven a desolate wild, autumn at the Dragon
    Treasure.
Night comes, wind and rain. Evil is a tough harvest.
If you talk "is/isn't" to other people,
You'll get paid back with Yunmen's "KAN!"

地老天荒龍寶秋
夜來風雨惡難收
對他若作是非話
彷彿雲門關字酬

2.

Samsara, "the suffering that comes of grasping," like fine red dust sifting into the eye—always abandon it. The fame of this one monk "Ikkyū"—always abandon it.

Daitō's successor, Ryōzen—his name means the Vulture Peak Mountain where Buddha taught two thousand years ago. The joyful beauty of Ryōzen's pure practice, strict monastic disciplines, always abandoning samsara.

But Ikkyū vowed never to abandon anyone lost in samsara. Never to hide in the mountains, never to discard the weapon of his fame.

Mara, king of all demons, waits for us on both sides of the road.

I'm ashamed that my reputation has not yet disappeared
After all this dusty work practicing Zen and studying dao.
Ryōzen's true dharma has been swept from the earth,
     extinguished.
A moment of inattention and the demon king is a hundred
     feet tall.

慚我聲名猶未韜
參禪學道長塵勞
靈山正法搜地滅
不意魔王十丈高

3.

The lineage of Ryōzen traces back through Daitō to Daitō's teacher's teacher, old Xutang. The bane of fraudulent monks, Xutang was slandered, one month jailed. In the collusion of officials, only an imperial reprieve got him out.

The ninth day of the ninth month is called Double Yang, when chrysanthemums reach their fullest bloom. That flower is also the family crest of the Japanese imperial house.

Old Xutang was imprisoned for one month,
And now Ikkyū's heart-broken body meets with misfortune.
Bitterness and pleasure, warm and cold, each season.
One cluster of yellow chrysanthemums, knowing Double
    Yang.

停囚一月老虛堂
身上迍遭休斷腸
苦樂寒溫箇時節
黃花一朵識重陽

4.

The world arises only from the purity of Buddha-mind—that wisdom and compassion is the root of everything. How then is this world filled with warfare? How has it become the screeching abode of the dead, a stinking corpse land, what the Chinese call the Yellow Springs? Only through unknowing, the preference for "is" or "isn't."

Lineage fathers, Ryōzen and before him Daitō and before him Xutang, these great warriors charged into the heart of war. "They mounted an iron horse and entered the citadel," says an old text, "those lineage founders who have passed through war, those generals operating outside the safe fortress."

A Zen teacher asked himself, "What is the correct time to wear a sword between your eyebrows?" And he answered himself, "When libation blood pours through the heavens of this world." After warfare, the Chinese make a purification offering to the spirits by pouring wine onto the ground.

poem #103

Purity, at its root, manifests the great one-thousand worlds.
Today's manifest world, the Yellow Springs.
Passing through war, the loyal red heart of the lineage
    founders appears everywhere.
When blood is poured through heaven, hang a sword
    between your eyebrows.

清淨本然現大千
現前境界是黃泉
慣戰作家赤心露
眉間掛劍血澆天

5.

In India it's said that once every hundred years, a bird flies over Mt. Meru, brushing the tallest peak with its wing. Each time, a bit of dust knocked off into the void. The time it takes the bird, and the bird's descendants, and theirs and theirs, to wear the mountain down is called a *kalpa*.

In the countryside, peasants carry manure in buckets slung from poles across their shoulders, fertilizer for the fields.

And Zhuangzi's "isn't" and "is." One night he dreamed he was a butterfly. Flitter flutter, he was a butterfly—he didn't know that he was Zhuang at all. Suddenly he woke up, Zhuang! He didn't know if he were Zhuang dreaming he was a butterfly, or a butterfly dreaming that it was Zhuang. This is called the transformation of things.

True transmission side-steps delusive combat.
Vast kalpas of unenlightenment are made of the feelings
    "self" and "other."
Carrying self and other makes the balance pole heavy.
When emptiness looks at a butterfly, the whole body becomes
    light.

正傳傍出妄相爭
曠刧無明人我情
人我担來担子重
空看蛺蝶一身輕

6.

The Seven Sages of the Bamboo Grove were drunk poets, music makers, and government officials who never compromised their decency. Xi Kang, master of the zither, would gather the other six at his home in Shanyang. Later he was executed for his integrity. When his heartmate Xiang Xiu learned of this, he smashed his own zither.

Later, passing by Shanyang, Xiu heard a countryman play the flute—the tone of that singular place. But by then his friend was dead, and only sound remained.

Antiquity's lustrous dao is bright these days–
People discussing the fame of Linji's true transmission.
Before my house, behind my house, everywhere the song of
    woodcutters.
I recall that ancient sound of the Shanyang flute.

上古道光今日明
議論臨濟正傳名
屋前屋後樵歌路
憶昔山陽笛一聲

7.

Zen Master Deshan jumped off the dais, grabbed his student, and beat him with a stick. Linji shouted and shouted in the monastery. Or stayed on his dais, not yelling, lecturing on the three essences and the three mysteries.

The King of Han, future founding Emperor of the Han dynasty, once found his army surrounded by enemy troops. Advisors urged him to forge the seals of other kings, fabricate a letter of support from them, and through this ruse escape. No, counseled another, through something very small, the seals, you will lose everything. So the Han king broke the seals, cracking them on the floor before him.

Old Xutang told this story afterwards. "Casting the Seal," his poem about meditation practice, and "Breaking the Seal," his poem of liberation, with the line "sleeping on a stone bed in the wilds." And *inka*, the "seal of enlightenment," that was given to Ikkyū on realization—he threw it off, and it was burned.

A commentator concludes: "Just practice meditation for another thirty years."

Stick and shout, the Zen of Deshan and Linji,
Debating the three essences and the three mysteries.
The Han King cast seals, then broke them.
Practice recklessly for another thirty years.

棒喝德山臨濟禪
商量三要與三玄
漢王鑄印卻消印
胡亂更參三十年

8.

Beyond reck and reckless: crazy cloud Ikkyū. Beyond is and isn't: Ikkyū's meditation of deep samadhi that never strays into the useless talk-dharma of fraudulent monks.

In Daitō's "Farewell Instructions" just before he died, he told his monks that though they may come to preside over golden temples with a thousand thousand students, if they lose the mystery-dao, then all dharma dies. "But," he said, "if a man stays living in the wild, passing his days in a reed hut, boiling wild vegetable roots in a broken-legged cook-pot, simply doing his meditation practice, then he and this old monk Daitō see each other every day, and he is the one who returns the kindness of my teaching."

This generation of long-practiced monks
Claims word-samadhi as their ability.
I have no ability, I have only flavor, a crazy-cloud house.
In the broken-legged cook-pot, one pint of rice.

近代久參學得僧
語言三昧喚為能
無能有味狂雲屋
折腳鐺中飯一升

9.

From his small mountain dwelling, the Tang poet Chu Sizong wrote:

> Downwind pine and cedar, the reckless mountains are green.
> Incense burning on a round table across from the stone
> screen.
> Empty, I recall how after last year's spring rain,
> Swallow droppings from time to time would stain *The Canon
> of Supreme Mystery.*

Huangbo, famous for his stick, teacher of Linji, contemporary of the poet Chu Sizong, once addressed the assembly:

> All you guys, all you drink is dregs. If you go on like this, wherever will today be?

And someone adds his comment:

> What are you using today for? Don't worry if you stir the multitude and alarm the crowd!

Linji used to say:

> Sometimes I take away the person but not the environment.
> Sometimes I take away the environment but not the person.
> Sometimes I take away both the person and the environment.
> Sometimes I take away neither the person nor the
> environment.

And those who followed him turned these sharp teaching tricks into four formal propositions, each standing for a higher stage of realization.

Downwind, pine and cedar recklessly enter the clouds.
Everywhere stir the multitude and alarm the crowd.
I can't do the tricks of "person" and "environment."
One cup of murky dregs gets me drunk drunk.

風外松杉亂入雲
諸方動眾又驚群
人境機關吾不會
濁醪一盞醉醺醺

IV.

Mori

——

whose name means "Forest"

Once a mountain spirit traveled to the southern rice terraces, answering the call of the King of Chu. There he dreamed her in the damp air, a shaman calling his spirit-lover from Shaman Mountain. She said, "I am just a guest here. I am the southern slope of the mountain. I brought you a pillow and mat." For one night they lay together as lovers. She never returned.

Her yin is a darkness: a reverie, the moon, companion to yang, which is the sun, his brightness. Her perfume: narcissus, called "the flower of nymphs." The poet Huang Tingjian wrote:

> Rising in the waves, the nymph wears dusty stockings.
> Atop the water, abundant, she follows the footsteps of the
>   tiny moon.

poem #535

A Beauty's Dark Yin Has the Scent of Narcissus

Behold the terraces of Chu and now climb them.
Half a night, sad colors of dream face on the jade bed.
The flower gives way beneath the branch of the plum tree.
Rising on the waves, the nymph wraps around my hips.

美人陰有仙花香

楚台應望更應攀
半夜玉床愁夢顏
花綻一莖梅樹下
凌波仙子遶腰間

The kōan of a poisonous snake in the deep southern mountains: "Take a good look at it," says the master, "all of you." And the commentator adds: "Its poisonous spirit wounds people."

At the same time as this kōan, two Tang monks in love went on a pilgrimage. They met a pregnant woman. One said in distress, "I made a vow to be born as her child. Now I must leave you to fulfill that obligation. But twelve years from now, meet me in a grove outside the India Temple."

Twelve years later, his companion heard a young cowherd singing in the moonlight:

I'm ashamed my lover had to come so far to meet me.
Though this body is different, my nature continually exists.

In late fall, Ikkyū heard Mori singing at the Yakushidō temple in the Sumiyoshi district of Sakai. Yakushidō, "Temple of the Medicine Buddha," the Buddha who heals all illness.

A Tang poet wrote:

The river wind penetrates the dawn, unable to sleep.
With the sound of all twenty-five zither strings, autumn
    complains of its lengthening nights.

poem #541

Talking Together at the Sumiyoshi Yakushidō
*On the 25th of November 1470 I traveled to the Yakushidō
and heard the blind woman's love ballads. So I made this
gatha to record it.*

With great ease and joy I traveled to the Yakushidō,

My belly full of poison spirit.

I'm ashamed that I don't notice my snow-frost topknot.

She chants till nothing's left, sharp cold complaint of

 lengthening nights.

住吉藥師堂并叙
 文明二年仲冬十四日遊藥師堂
 聽盲女豔歌因作偈記之

優遊且熹藥師堂

毒氣便便是我腸

愧慚不管雪霜鬢

吟盡嚴寒愁點長

Ikkyū had been alone in Takigi, south of the capital, open fields and bamboo forest.

His ancient vow of solitude. Then, avoiding war, he moved to Sumiyoshi.

Li Bo, exuberant poet of Tang China, master of fūryū, was always longing for something, fame, favor, wine, his home, the moon. Sometimes he takes on the voice of a court lady waiting for love:

White dew emerging on the jade steps.
Night lengthens, creeps into my stockings.
I withdraw, lowering the water-crystal curtains.
In the sound of their chiming, I look toward the autumn
    moon.

I remember when I lived in the Takigi countryside.

As soon as we heard each other's name, we imagined each
other.

Now that the vow of many years is forgotten,

I love the new moon's shape on jade steps even more.

*Regarding the above, I dwelt for some years in a small
cottage in Takigi. The attendant Mori had heard of my
manner and was intent on her love for me. I also knew
of this but hesitated until now. In the spring of 1471, we
met by chance in Sumiyoshi. I asked about her intent,
and she responded favorably. So I made this small poem
to tell of it.*

憶昔薪園居住時

王孫美譽聽相思

多年舊約即妄後

更愛玉墀新月姿

右余寓薪園小舍有年森侍者聞
余風采已有嚮慕之志余亦知焉
然因循至今辛卯之春邂逅于墨
吉問以索志則諾而應因作小詩
述之

Zen Master Huanglong, "The Yellow Dragon," would stop students at his Three Barriers—three questions that halt conceptual mind. The commentator observes: "If you don't pass through the patriarch's barrier, if you don't cut off your mind-stream, you are not even a free-agent ghost, you're still caught haunting grasses and trees."

The Second Barrier asks: "How does my hand resemble the Buddha's hand?" One hand grabs another and everybody feels it, one ailment and everyone is ill. Yet before everything there is Mori, master of the secret assembly that is Ikkyū's own body.

poem #536

Calling My Hand Mori's Hand

How does my hand resemble Mori's hand?
I believe the lady is a fūryū master.
When I'm sick, she makes my jade stalk sprout,
Delighting all in my assembly.

喚我手作森手

我手何似森手
自信公風流主
發病治玉莖萌
且熹我會裡眾

Yang Guifei, consort of the Tang Emperor, was one of the Four Beauties of ancient China. The Emperor compared her to crab-apple flowers, *haitang*, "the ocean cherry-apple." He loved her especially when she was slightly drunk, singing, swaying, and he'd feed her sweets, placing them into her mouth.

They met when the Emperor was in his fifties, she not yet twenty. He named the last fourteen years of his reign Tianbao, "Heaven's Treasure," perhaps for her. Years of spring love-making, and then disaster.

The name Mori means "forest," a pictogram of three trees 森.

Watching the Beauty Mori Nap at Noon

A beauty who is the fūryū of the age.
Luxurious love ballads, pure feasts, exquisitely new songs.
I chant a new poem to her heart-breaking flower-face
　　dimples.
Mori, you're a heaven-treasure, ocean-apple, you're a whole
　　forest of blooming trees.

看森美人午睡

一代風流之美人
豔歌清宴曲尤新
新吟斷腸花顔靨
天寶海棠森樹春

Regarding a Painting of Ikkyū and Mori Together in a Single Scroll, Dated Winter 1471

Fifth year of the Ōnin War. Daitoku-ji, all northern Kyōtō, just rubble and ash. Monks dispersed, pavilions and brothels empty, shops closed, plague in the streets. And in the west, impoverished peasants tumbling into revolt. Always on the move—starvation, skeletons walking everywhere.

The Pavilion Monk Ikkyū looks like Xutang, the great Chinese antecedent of Daitoku-ji. His mind fully occupies the Great Circle that is all the heavens.

On this portrait, Ikkyū's poem and Mori's poem written in Ikkyū's own hand.

Within the face of the great circle, the whole body
   manifests—
The painting shows the truth of Xutang's face and eyes.
The blind woman's love ballads mock the Pavilion Monk.
Her one song before flowers, ten-thousand years of spring.

大圓相裏現全身

劃出虛堂面目真

盲女豔歌笑樓子

花前一曲萬年春

Song of the Exalted Lady Mori

Heavy, thought-filled sleep
on a bed of sleep, floating,
floating and sinking.
Waves of tears: except for these
I have no joy or pleasures.

森上郎の御詠

おもいねの
うきねのとこに
うきしずむ
なみだならでは
なぐさみもなし

The red-plumed phoenix is often joined in union with her mate.

A phoenix carriage, the royal conveyance, bears the Emperor through land and sky. "It must be made with reverence," writes the ancient scholar Dongzhong Shu. "It is modeled on the ordering of Heaven, it is drawn by a team of four phoenixes."

Zhuangzi wandered, floating through spring.

Lady Mori Rides by Carriage

In spring, the blind woman often wanders in her phoenix
　　carriage.
It pleases her to soothe my autumn gloom.
Despite the mocking of all beings,
I love to look at Mori, her lovely fūryū.

森公乘輿

鸞輿盲女屢春遊
鬱鬱胸襟好慰秋
遮莫眾生之輕賤
愛看森也美風流

Guishan's *Admonitions* from late Tang still shapes the rules of all earnest practice. He'd say, "You old monks, if you're not attentive, a hundred years from now I'll be reborn as a water-buffalo down the mountain." His monks' fear of rebirth as a stupid animal, with no chance of enlightenment. Their striving for incarnation as a human being, again and again.

Yet the human body is also something for monks to fear. Once a Chinese goddess took rocks to buttress heaven against *yin*, "a surfeit of water." Often the flooding of the north China plain sweeps all barriers to sea. And always, like its cognate *yin*, "the lewdness of humans," the flood of desire rises to engulf the body.

Guishan's contemporary Yantou relates the story of two monks. At the start of the summer training session, their master had only said to them, "What's this?" and then walked away.

> Yantou said, "Ah, how I regret now that in that moment I didn't give the 'final words' that would have completed things."
>
> Three months later the monks told Yantou that they hadn't understood his comment.
>
> "Why didn't you ask me earlier?" demanded Yantou.
>
> "We didn't dare to," they said.

A commentator remarks: "If you monks aren't willing to dare to, how can I secretly report these words to you?" "Secret report": a privileged communication to the Emperor. If you monks aren't willing to dare to, how will you ever hear the secret report of your liberation?

The "private words at midnight" that the Tang Emperor exchanged with Yang Guifei, vowing to be reborn together as two wings of a single bird, vowing to be reborn together in all three lives of past, present, and future.

poem #529

Drinking the Waters of a Beauty's Wet Sex

Secret report: I'm ashamed of our league of private words.
As our fūryū singing ends, we take the three-lives vow.
Our flesh-bodies will fall into the animal realm.
How marvelous, this feeling of Guishan wearing horns!

吸美人婬水

密啟自慚私語盟
風流吟罷約三生
生身墮在畜生道
絕勝溈山戴角情

During the Ōnin War, Yamana Sōzen, the Red-Faced Monk, cut off all deliveries of rice to Kyōtō. The Emperor could not prevent it. This starvation spread into the surrounding countryside.

Fifteen hundred years earlier, in China, briefly a truce with the western nomads. The Chinese Emperor sent Su Wu out as ambassador. Yet abruptly conditions changed. The nomads imprisoned Su Wu and demanded he switch sides. But he would not betray his Emperor. They stuck him in an underground cell with no food or water, but he ate the fur off his robes and drank snow that melted down the walls. He was exiled to steppe-land a thousand miles west and, when food was gone, ate wild grasses and rodents. Still, he would not submit. Nineteen years later he was rescued and returned to China.

Zen Master Baizhang would rarely offer the expected formal discourse or public ceremony, saying, "Oh tomorrow, oh tomorrow." Instead he sent his monks to farm, telling them "A day not working is a day not eating." Patrons drifted off, nothing there for them. And still his Zen students kept on tilling their fields and feeding their monasteries.

The Indians call the Lord of Death "Yama," the judge with a red face. The kōan says,

> When old Yama asks, "Do you want any rice money?" you should know how many straw sandals he's tromped around in.

Yama has been around longer than anyone; he's worn out more pairs of straw sandals than Su Wu ate blades of grass.

Su Wu, loyal to the end, vomited blood when his Emperor died and was buried outside the capital at Maoling. A Tang poet wrote:

> Who will provision Su Wu on the final return to his country?
> Maoling pine and cedar, rain sound plok-plok.

During the famine, Mori gave her food to Ikkyū, the Pavilion Monk, insisting that he eat instead of her. The King of Chu was fed by his consort in a dream.

The blind woman, Mori, my attendant, has generous feel-
ings of love. She is going to starve herself to death. Over-
come with grief, I made this gatha to speak of it.

Baizhang's hoe made patrons' gifts melt away.
Yama hasn't been generous with the rice money.
The blind woman's love ballads mock the Pavilion Monk.
Chu terrace, evening rain dripping plok-plok.

盲女森侍者情愛甚厚將絕食殞命愁苦之余作偈言之

百丈鋤頭信施消
飯錢閻老不曾饒
盲女豔歌咲樓子
楚台暮雨滴蕭蕭

The Buddha was considered complete and perfect, the only refuge, until the Third Zen Patriarch Sengcan wrote the "Inscription on Confidence in Mind," overthrowing the dependency on Buddha. Don't rely on Buddha, Buddha is only mind, one's own mind, there is nothing external to achieve. His inscription begins:

The very dao is without difficulties,
Only it rejects choosing.
Just don't hate and love:
Piercingly clear!

And then that clear mind was considered complete and perfect, the only refuge, until Zhaozhou rose up:

Zhaozhou instructed the assembly, saying "'The very dao is without difficulties, only it rejects choosing.' Yet as soon as there is speaking, that is 'choosing,' that is 'clarity.'"

There is no Buddha to be confident in, no mind to speak of, no words to speak with, and no clarity. There is nothing internal to achieve. And so the kōan commentator elaborates, "To say 'the very dao is without difficulties'—that's a mouthful of hard frost."

And this silence was considered complete and perfect. Yet still, plum trees blooming in the snow.

The Song dynasty hermit Lin Bu spent twenty years in a cottage on Solitary Isle. Plum trees were his wives and concubines, the cranes his children. He wrote of them:

Spare shadows slant
    the waters pure and shallow,
Dim fragrance floats
    the moon at yellow dusk.

The Waters of Her Sex

A dream deceives me: the beauty Mori in the Royal Gardens.
News of opening flowers on her pillow, plum blossoms
    confident in mind.
Mouth full of pure fragrance, of pure shallow water.
In yellow dusk, the moon-color of sex, how could I make a
    new song?

婬水

夢迷上苑美人森
枕上梅花花信心
滿口清香清淺水
黃昏月色奈新吟

Among the *Nineteen Old Poems* of Han is this verse:

Floating clouds cover the white sun.
The distant traveler does not turn to look back.

In "Bequeathing a Hermitage to a Monk Friend," the Tang poet Sikong Tu writes:

There are obstacles to returning to the ancient mountain,
But don't delay for that.

All journeys end at Yellow Springs, the land of death. And then begin again.

poem #A79

Still in the Boudoir, My Return to the Temple Delayed

Distant traveler, Dream Boudoir, misses the time of his
    return—
Increasing pains, sad songs, more sickness.
This monk wandering to Yellow Springs has one regret:
That to see and meet you again should always be so delayed.

閨中歸寺遲

夢閨遊子誤歸期
添苦愁吟多病時
只恨黃泉行腳路
相看再會總遲遲

At the River Xiang, Shun's two widows mourned themselves to death. Their tears turned to blood, their unending passion turned to unending grief, and so they became the ghosts of that river.

For one endless night the King of Chu met his shaman lover. When he looked for her the next morning, he found only mountain mist. Then for an endless eternity she was gone. He seeks her always now in the clouds and rain, their two bodies drenched in love.

In Celebration of the Return of Dream Boudoir and His
Woman Attendant to the Temple

Three days apart feels like an eternal kalpa,
Tears and rain of the Xiang River pouring through my chest.
Outside Dream Boudoir's curtains: the moon at the tip of a
    pine branch.
Mountain hut, the night is deep. You sing together with me.

賀夢閨姑侍者歸寺

三日別離永刧心
湘江淚雨洒胸襟
夢閨簾外松梢月
山舍夜深君共吟

The ancient kōan text:

A monk asked Yunmen, "What's it like when the tree withers
and leaves fall?"
Yunmen said, "Body completely exposed to autumn's golden
wind."

In another kōan:

The withered tree again blooms,
Bodhidharma roams the eastern lands.

An early Tang poet wrote:

This road where we part goes on a thousand miles and more.
Your profound blessings will weigh on me a hundred years.

poem #543

Written Out of Desire to Thank Lady Mori for Her Profound
Blessings

The tree withers, leaves fall. Spring returns again.
The long green stems give birth to flowers, old vows are
    renewed.
Ah Mori, your profound blessings. If I forget and turn away,
For a million measureless kalpas I'll be born again and again
    as an animal.

謝森公深恩之願書

木稠葉落更回春
長綠生花舊約新
森也深恩若忘卻
無量億刧畜生身

The monk Huiyue preached dharma in the wilds. A tiger rested its head on his knee, making a pillow.

An imperial concubine of the Jin dynasty often dreamed she saw two dragons resting their heads on each other's knees, as the sun and moon entered their breasts.

Poem on Leaving This World

For ten years beneath abundant flowers, we wove the texture
　　of our life.
One span of fūryū, limitless feelings.
I can't bear parting—man, woman, resting our heads on each
　　other's knees.
Nights deep with cloud and rain, our vow of all three lives.

辭世詩

十年花下理芳盟
一段風流無限情
惜別枕頭兒女膝
夜深雲雨約三生

The center of the world is Mt Meru. To the south is India, Bud-dha's homeland and the origin of this dharma, to the east China, and across the sea from that, Japan. Seven generations ago in China, Xutang began the lineage that would found Daitoku-ji, its temple and monastery burned to the ground in the Ōnin War.

Afterwards, the Emperor asked Ikkyū to rebuild it. He never fin-ished. When he was sick and about to die, his disciples carried him on a palanquin to his hut in the bamboo forest, then carried him back.

South of Mt Meru,
Who can meet my Zen?
The coming of Xutang
Isn't worth a dime.
—Pure Ikkyū of the Eastern Sea

須弥南畔

誰會我禪

虛堂來也

不直十錢
東海純一休

Notes and References

These notes give quick identity to the poetry and stories mentioned in our introduction to each poem. Well-known works are usually cited in English, less common or untranslated works in Chinese. The name "Hirano" refers to his edition of Ikkyū's poems, whose full bibliographic reference is in our Introduction. "T" indicates the Taishō *Tripitika*, "Z" the *Zokuzōkyō*. All Chinese works can be found online.

Poem

5
Zhuangzi, ch 15
巖頭，睦州
Record of Linji, "Discourses," section 10

23
傳燈錄, ch 11, 鄧州
Record of Linji, "Discourses" section 18

90
蘇軾 et al, from tieba.baidu.com/f?kz=606876736, response of 吧友
124.131.217
佛鑒, in 人天眼目
傳燈錄, ch 19

100
Zhuangzi, ch 2
Blue Cliff Record, case 8

102
陶潛, "飲酒詩之五"
Ikkyū, poem #332

103
Blue Cliff Record, case 24
昭覺元, 五燈會元, ch 19

104
Zhuangzi, ch 2

105
晉書, ch 49

106
史記, 留侯世家, ch 55
虛堂, "钁印" and "消印," quoted in Hirano
Blue Cliff Record, case 20

107
大燈國師の遺誡

108
儲嗣宗, "和茅山高遺拾山中雜題五首。小樓"
Blue Cliff Record, case 11
Record of Linji, "Discourses," section 10

123
Record of Linji, "Discourses," sections 10 and 9
六組壇經
Ikkyū, poem #54

125
Record of Linji, "Record of Pilgrimages," sections 22 and 1
圜悟克勤
梁武帝, "一段風光畫不成"

144
黃庭堅, "鷓鴣天。明日獨酌自嘲呈史應之"
禪宗雜毒海, ch 3

151
顧況, "捨山中"
白居易, "宿竹閣"
Record of Linji, "Record of Pilgrimages," section 2

156
Record of Linji, "Critical Examinations," section 6
Blue Cliff Record, case 9

208
Blue Cliff Record, case 91
六組壇經

255
Lankavatara Sutra, T0945.19. 0106c

259
五燈會元, ch 6
禪林僧寶傳, ch 21

260
白居易, "長恨歌"
Zhuangzi, ch 2
無門關, ch 8
二十二祖摩拏罗, 佛光大辞典

271
禮記, "樂記"

304
雜寶蔵經, ch 3
李白, "白紵辭"

309
廣慧, 傳燈錄, ch 30

329
史記, "辟陽侯," ch 97
范摅, 雲溪友議
李群玉 , "湘妃廟"

340
Record of Linji, "Record of Pilgrimages," section 21
五祖, Z65, No. 1295, 禪宗頌古聯珠通集
Vimalakirti, T0475.14.0548

421
禪林類聚, ch 19, Z117
五燈會元, ch 4

454
"咿啞聲裡暗颦眉," 南宋, anonymous

477
Record of Linji, "Critical Examinations," section 18
Blue Cliff Record, case 32

489
丁福保, 佛學大辭典,百丈禪師, lines 1, 3, 4 and 8
Record of Linji, "Record of Pilgrimages," section 9

495
Record of Linji, "Record of Pilgrimages," section 21
Blue Cliff Record, case 49
Ikkyū, poem #819

508
Blue Cliff Record, case 24
圓覺經, T842.17

529
Blue Cliff Record, case 24
曹植, "女媧贊"
Blue Cliff Record, case 51
白居易, "長恨歌"

531
漢書, 蘇武傳
Blue Cliff Record, case 66
五燈會元, ch 6
李商隱, "茂陵"

533
董仲舒, "春秋繁露‧三代改制"

534
僧璨, "信心銘"
Blue Cliff Record, case 2
林逋, "山園小梅"

535
黃庭堅, "王充道送水仙花"

536
五燈會元, ch 17

541
Blue Cliff Record, case 22
袁郊, "甘澤遙"
李郢, "宿杭州虛白堂"

542
李白, "玉階怨"

543
Blue Cliff Record, case 27
Blue Cliff Record, case 2
王勃, "秋日別王長史"

615
Record of Linji, "Record of Pilgrimages," section 1
Record of Linji, "Discourses," section 10
"Skeletons," in Hirano

823
Blue Cliff Record, case 46
Zhuangzi, ch 15
尹鶚, "滿宮花"
杜甫, "月夜"

A79
古詩十九首, "行行重行行"
司空圖, "僧舍貽友人"

A158
法苑珠林, ch 81
晉書,后妃傳下,孝武文李太后

"Enlightenment"
四十二章經, sec 24
昭陽宮, see 王昌齡, "長信怨"

"Portrait"
from Hirano, vol 5, p 72

"South of Mt Meru"
from Hirano, vol 5, p 98

Further Reading

Sonja Arntzen. Ikkyū and the Crazy Cloud Collection. New York and Tokyo: Columbia University Press and Tokyo University Press, 1986.

Jon Carter Covell and Yamada Sōbin. Zen at Daitoku-ji. Tokyo: Kodansha International, 1974.

Donald Keene. "The Portrait of Ikkyū." Archives of Asian Art, 20 (1966–67), 54–65.

David Pollack. Zen Poems of the Five Mountains. New York: The Crossroads Publishing Company and Scholars Press, 1985.

Peipei Qiu. "Aesthetic of Unconventionality: Fūryū in Ikkyū's poetry." Japanese Language and Literature, 35.2 (Oct 2001), 135–56.

James Sanford. Zen-Man Ikkyū. Harvard University Studies in World Religions. Chico, CA: Scholars Press, 1981.

John Stevens. Wild Ways. Buffalo, NY: White Pine Press, 2007.

Marian Ury. Poems of the Five Mountains: An Introduction to the Literature of the Zen Monasteries. Ann Arbor, MI: Michigan Monograph Series in Japanese Studies, No 10, 1992.

Authors

Sarah Messer is the author of two books of poetry, *Bandit Letters* (New Issues) and *Dress Made of Mice* (Black Lawrence Press) and a hybrid memoir, *Red House* (Viking/Penguin). She has received grants and awards from the National Endowment for the Arts, Mellon Foundation, the Fine Arts Work Center in Provincetown, the Wisconsin Institute for Creative Writing, and the Radcliffe Institute (Bunting) at Harvard University.

For many years **Kidder Smith** taught Chinese history at Bowdoin College, where he also chaired the Asian Studies Program. He is the senior author of *Sung Dynasty Use of the I Ching* (Princeton) and, with the Denma Translation Group, of *Sun Tzu—The Art of War* (Shambhala).

Afterword

Ikkyū was never angry. His mother was never sent to Long Gate Palace. He never heard a crow. None the less. . . .

Photo: Sarah Messer